Trains Adults Coloring Book: Transportation Coloring Book Vol.1

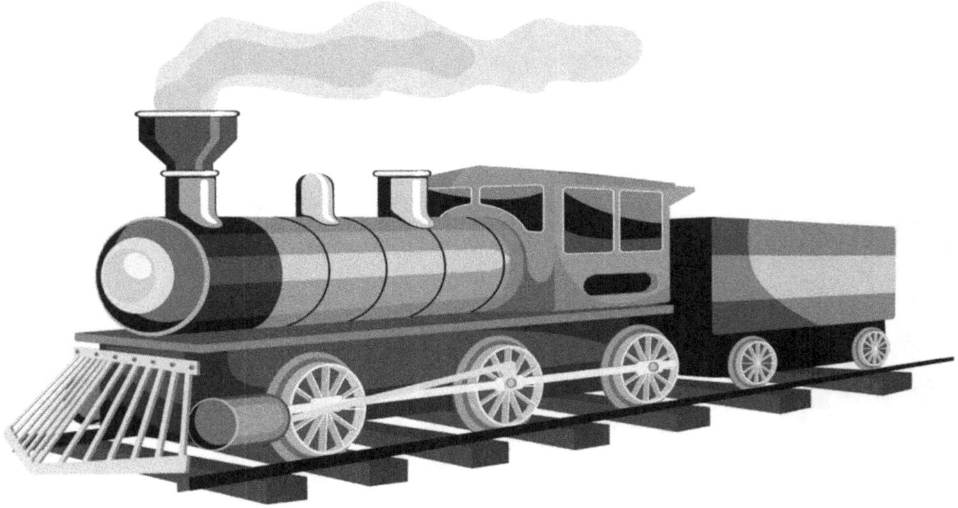

Baizy pubshing

Trains Adults Coloring Book: Transportation Coloring Book Vol.1

Copyright: Published in the United States by baizy publishing
Published November 2016

ISBN-13:978-1540385451

ISBN-10:1540385450

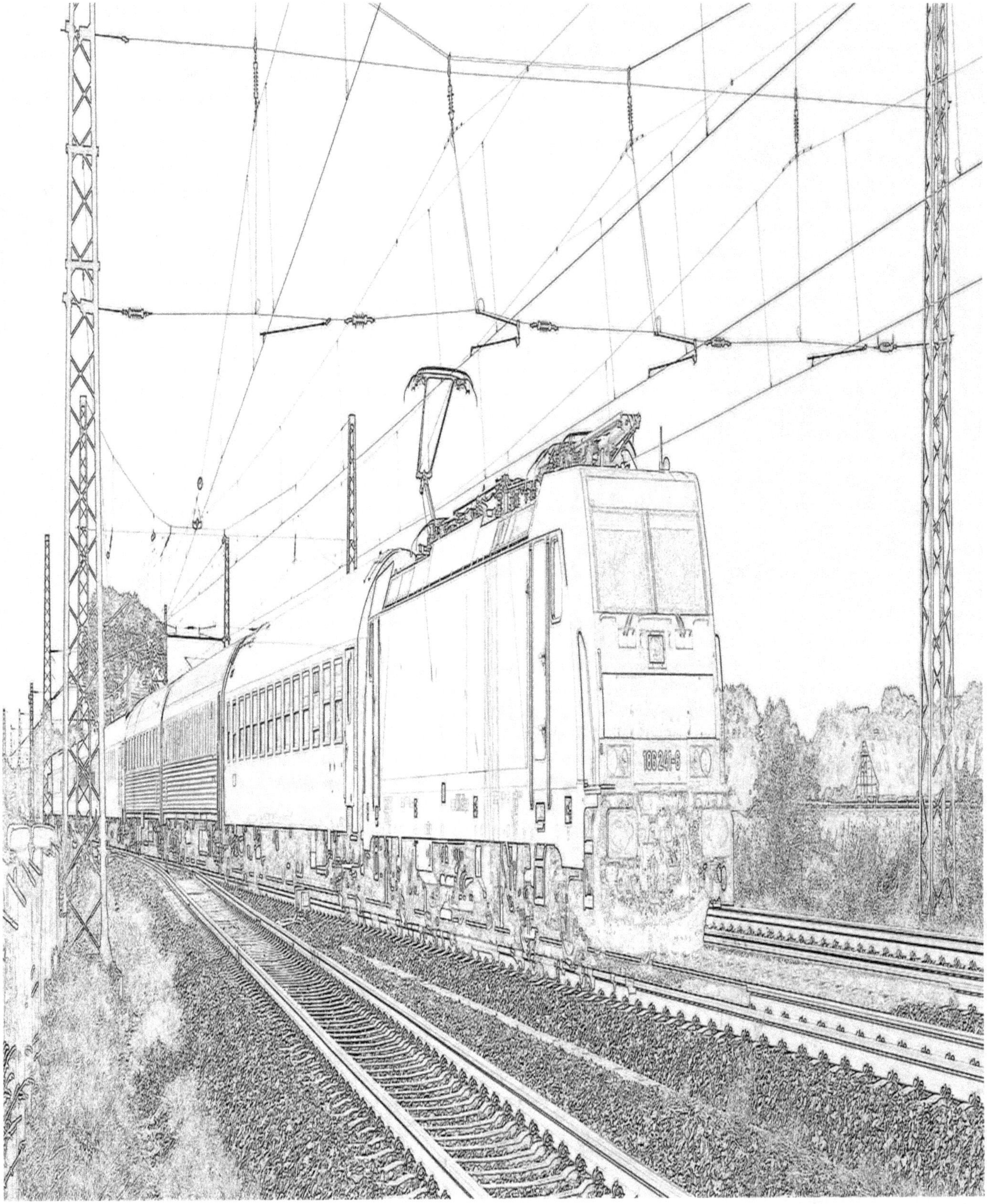
186 241-6

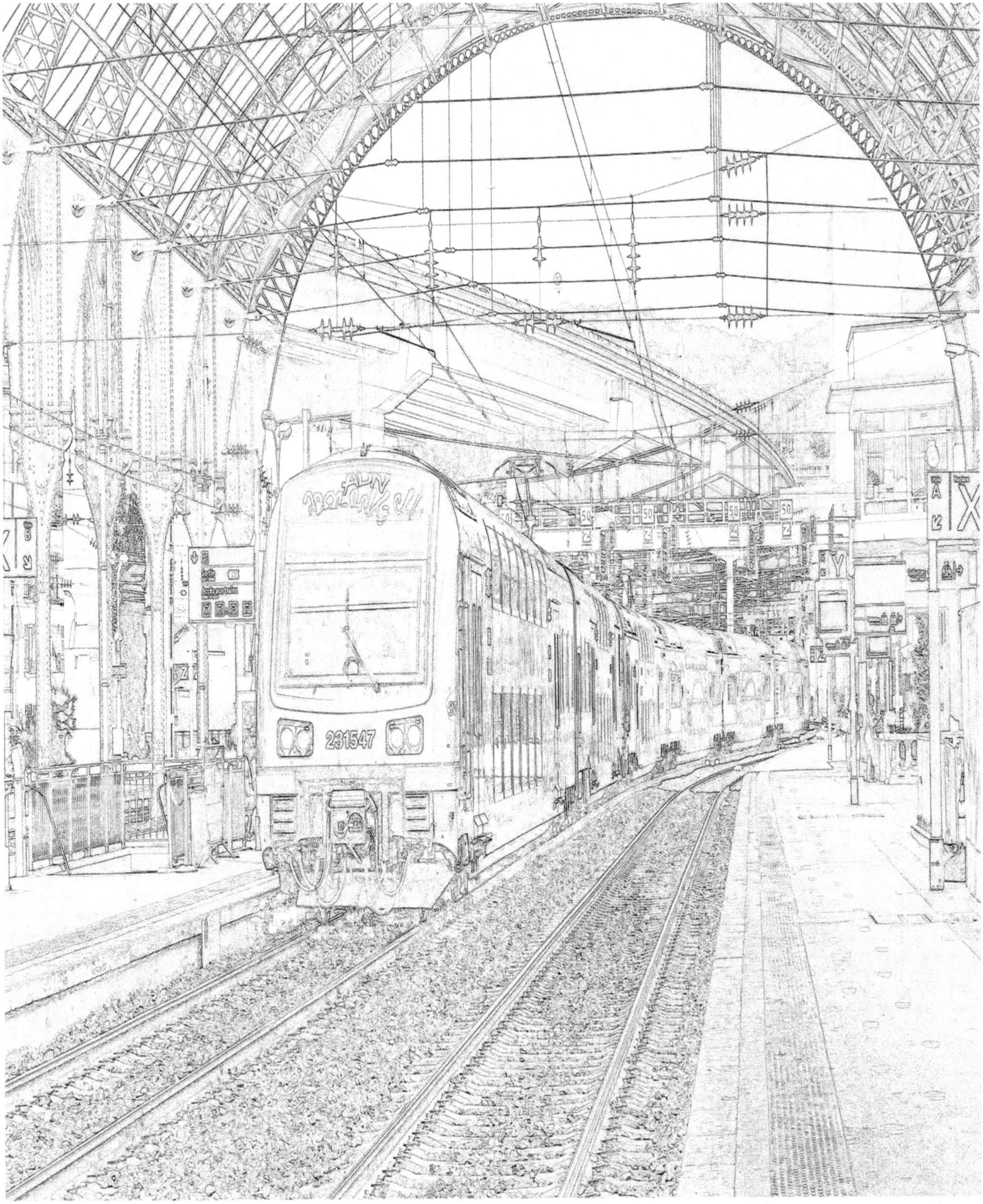
231547

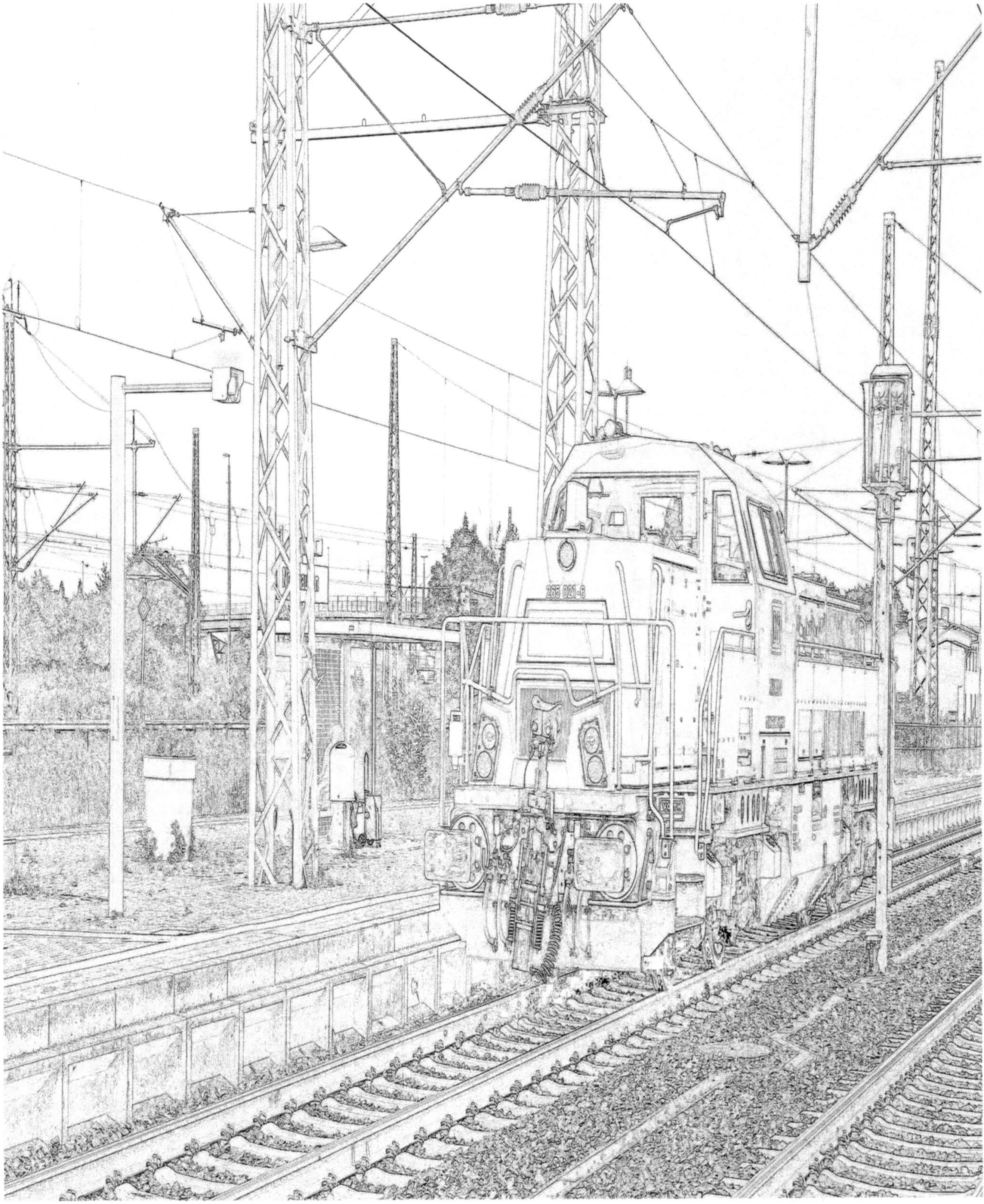
265 021-6
VOITH

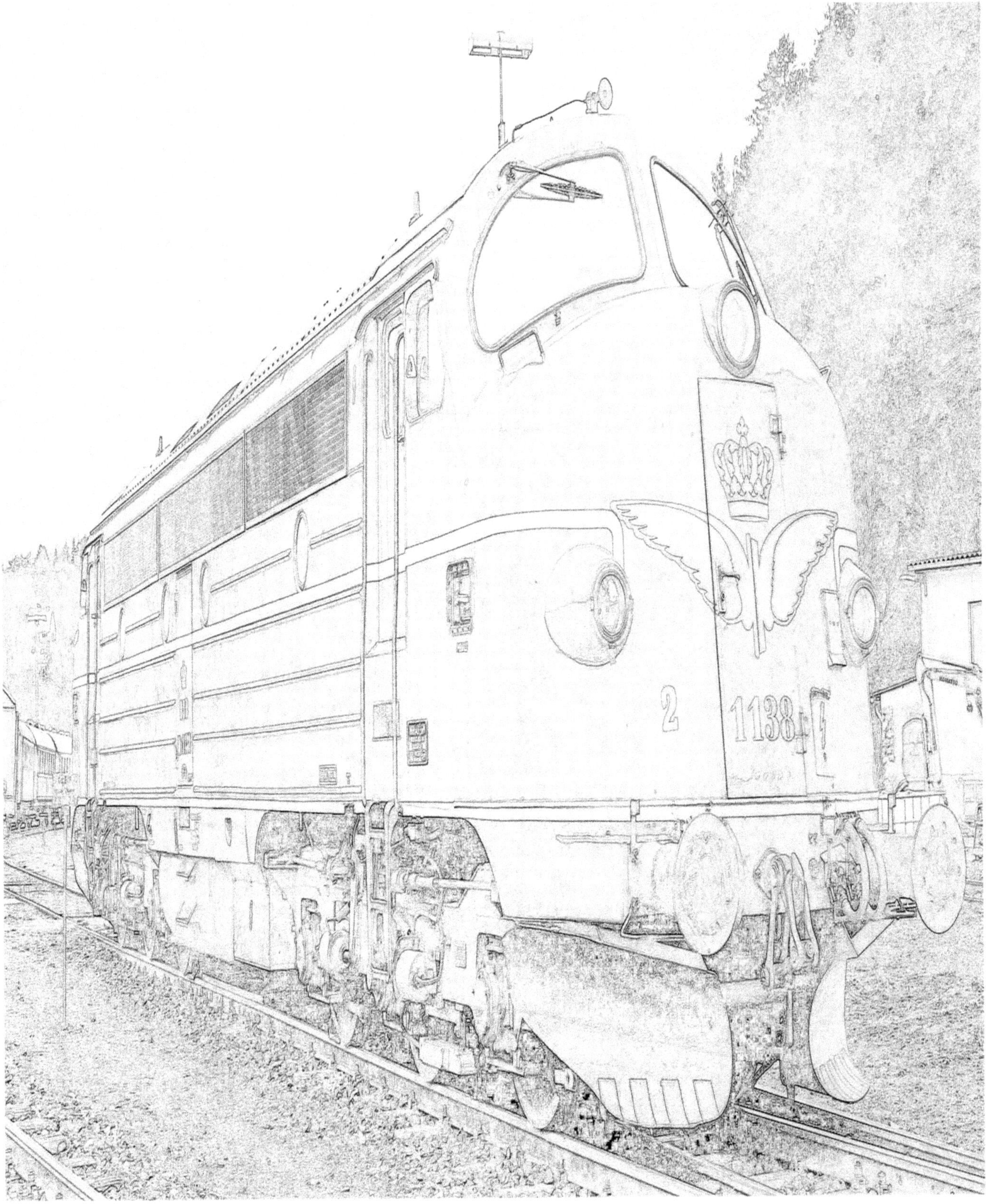
2
1138

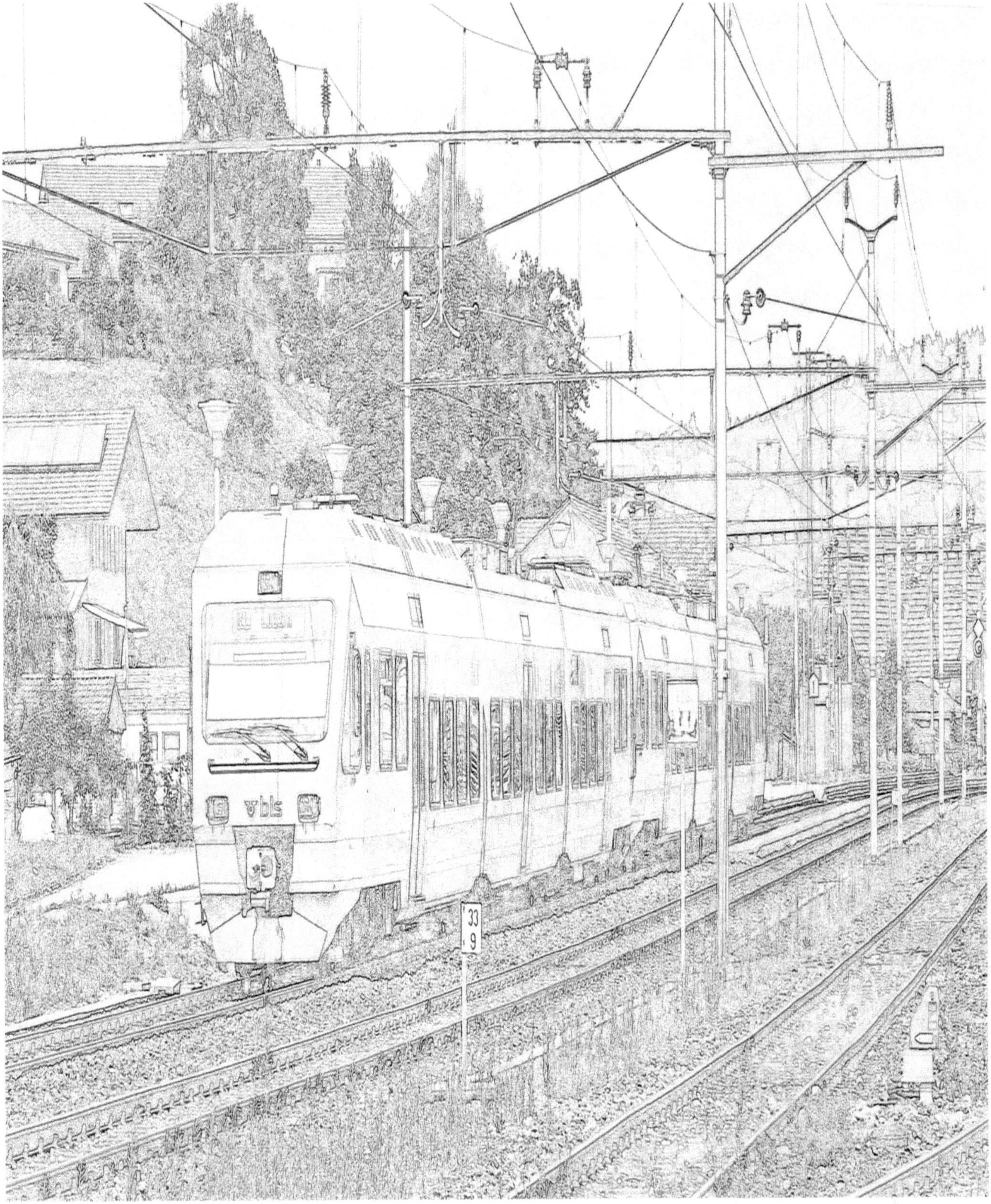
bls
33
9

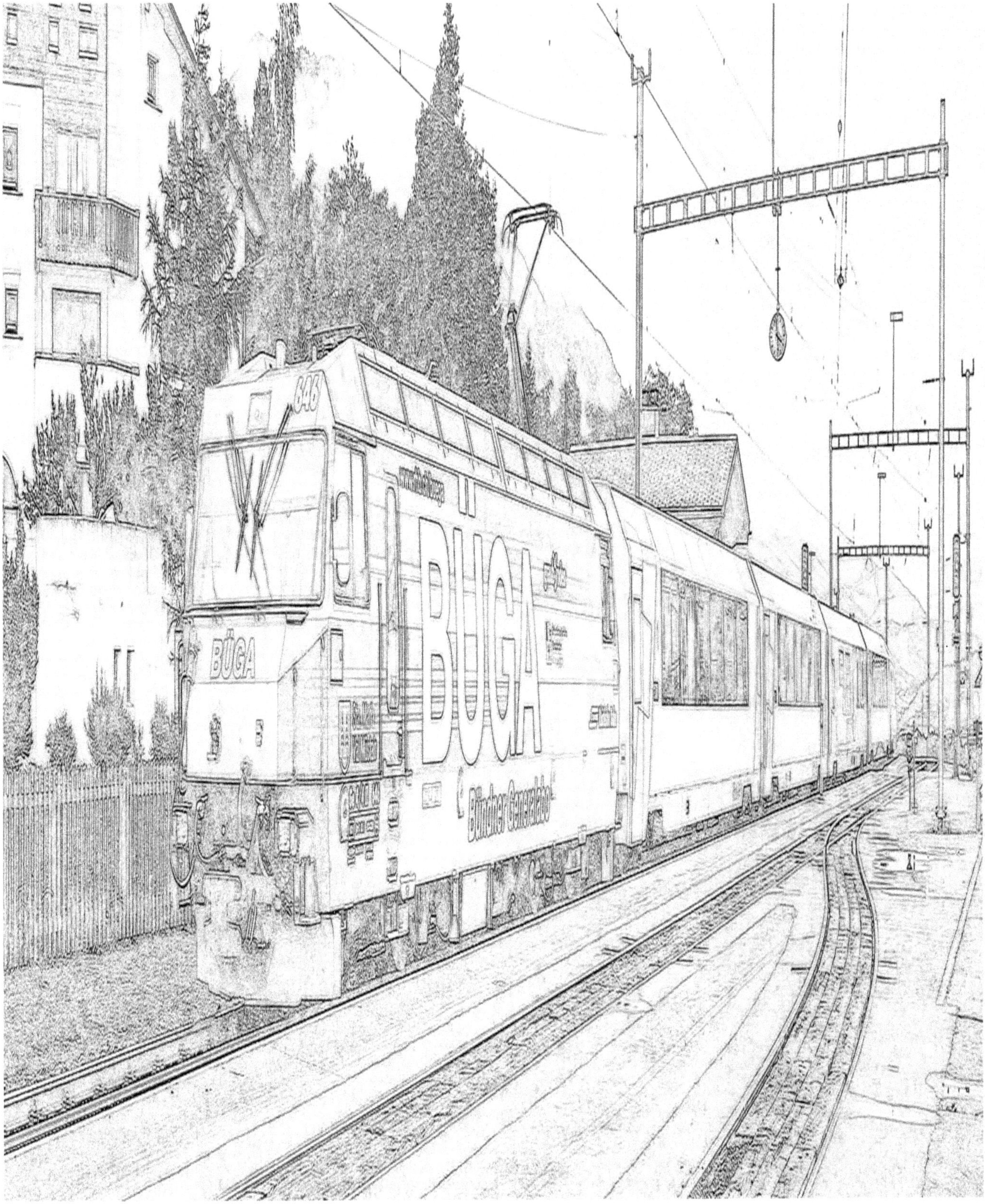
648
BÜGA
BÜGA
Bündner Generalabo

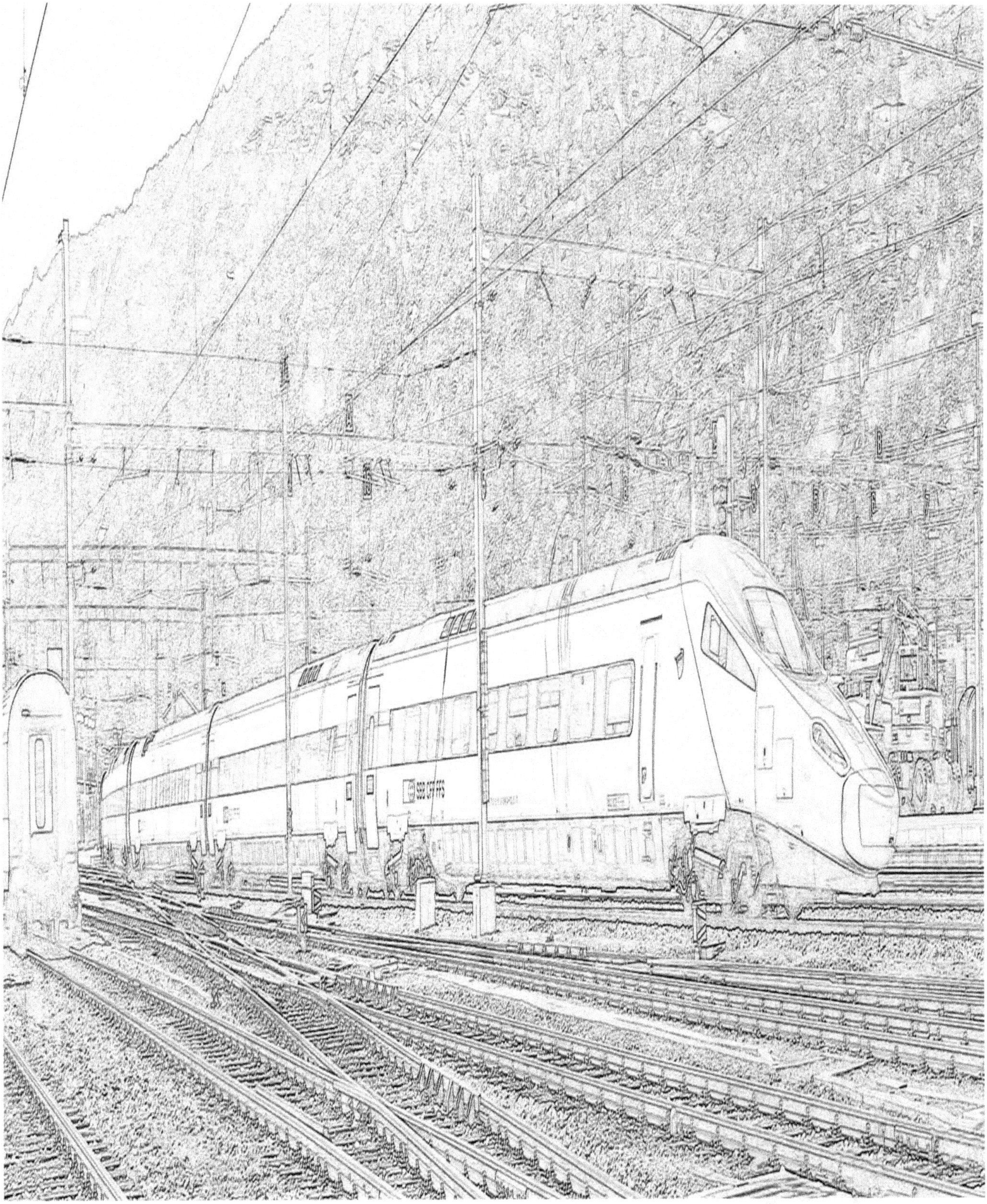
SBB CFF FFS

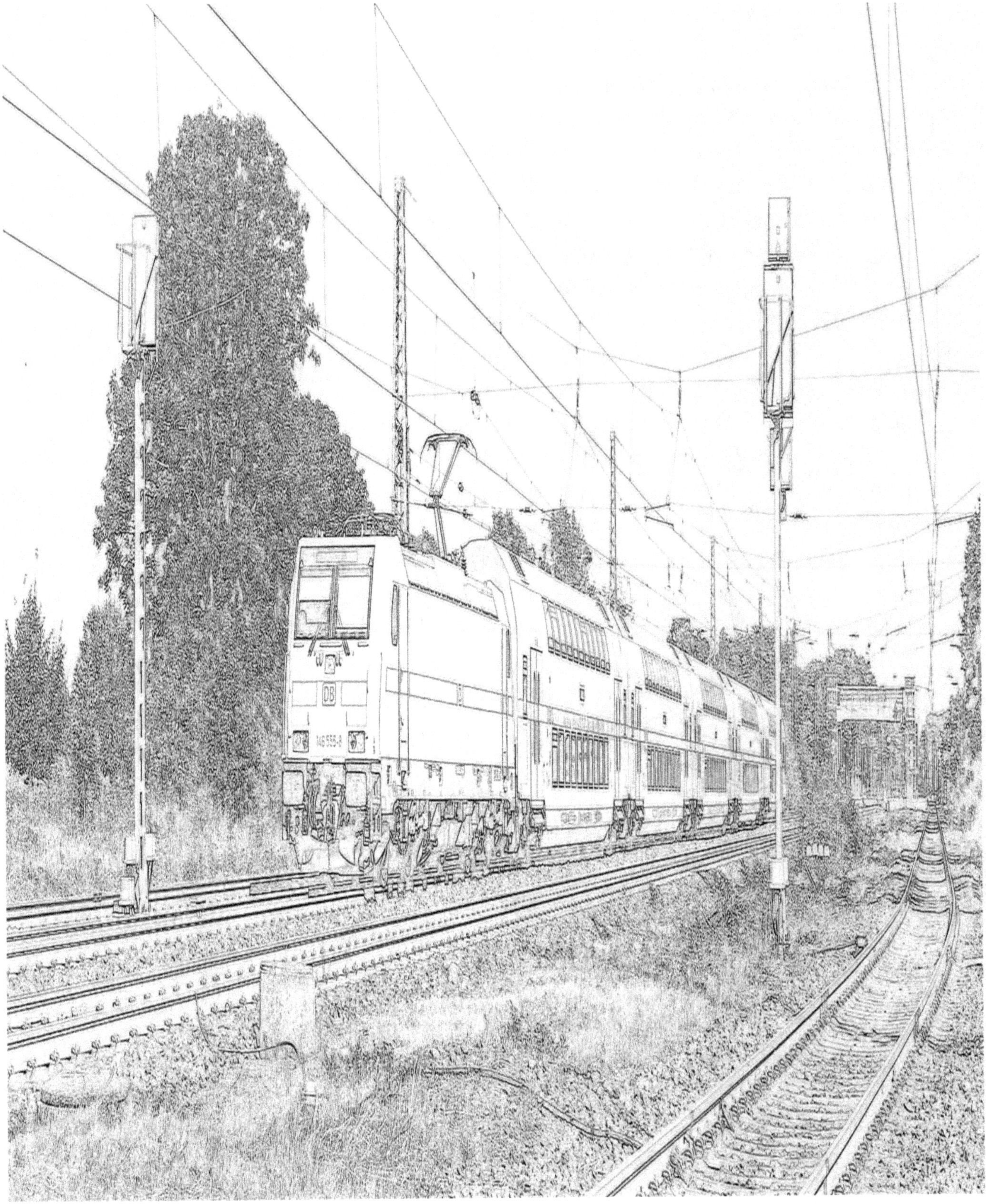

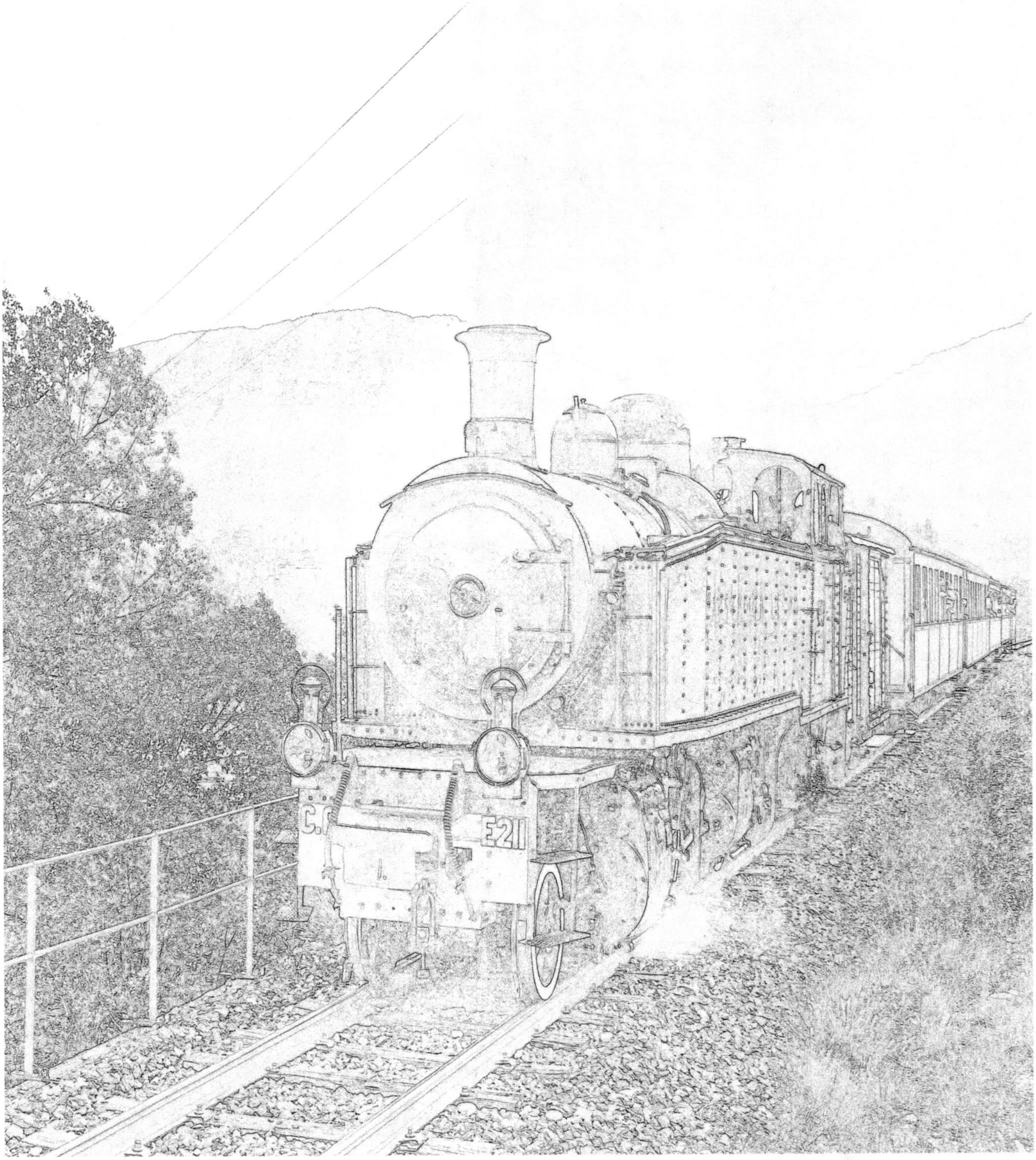
E211

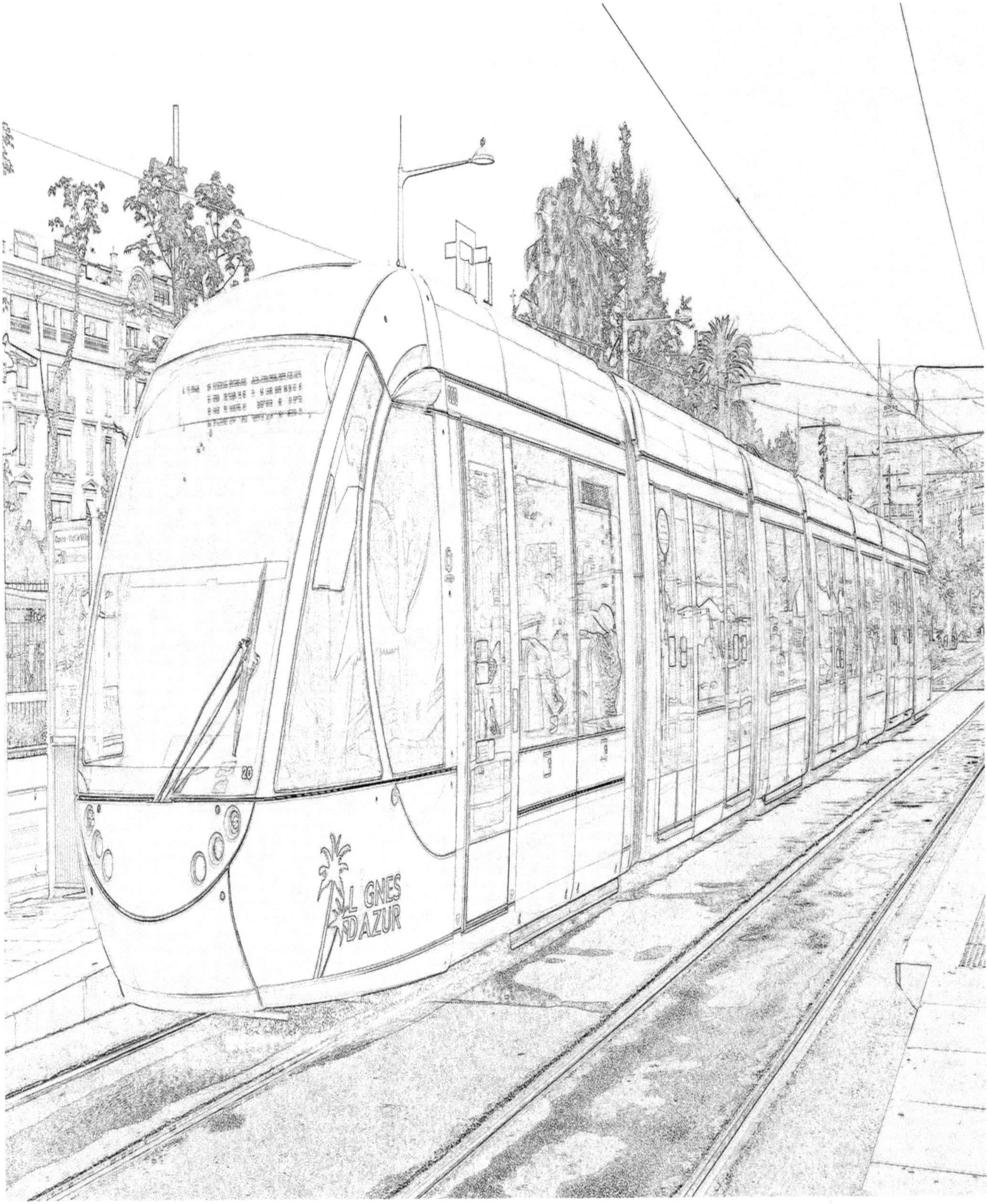
L GNES
DAZUR

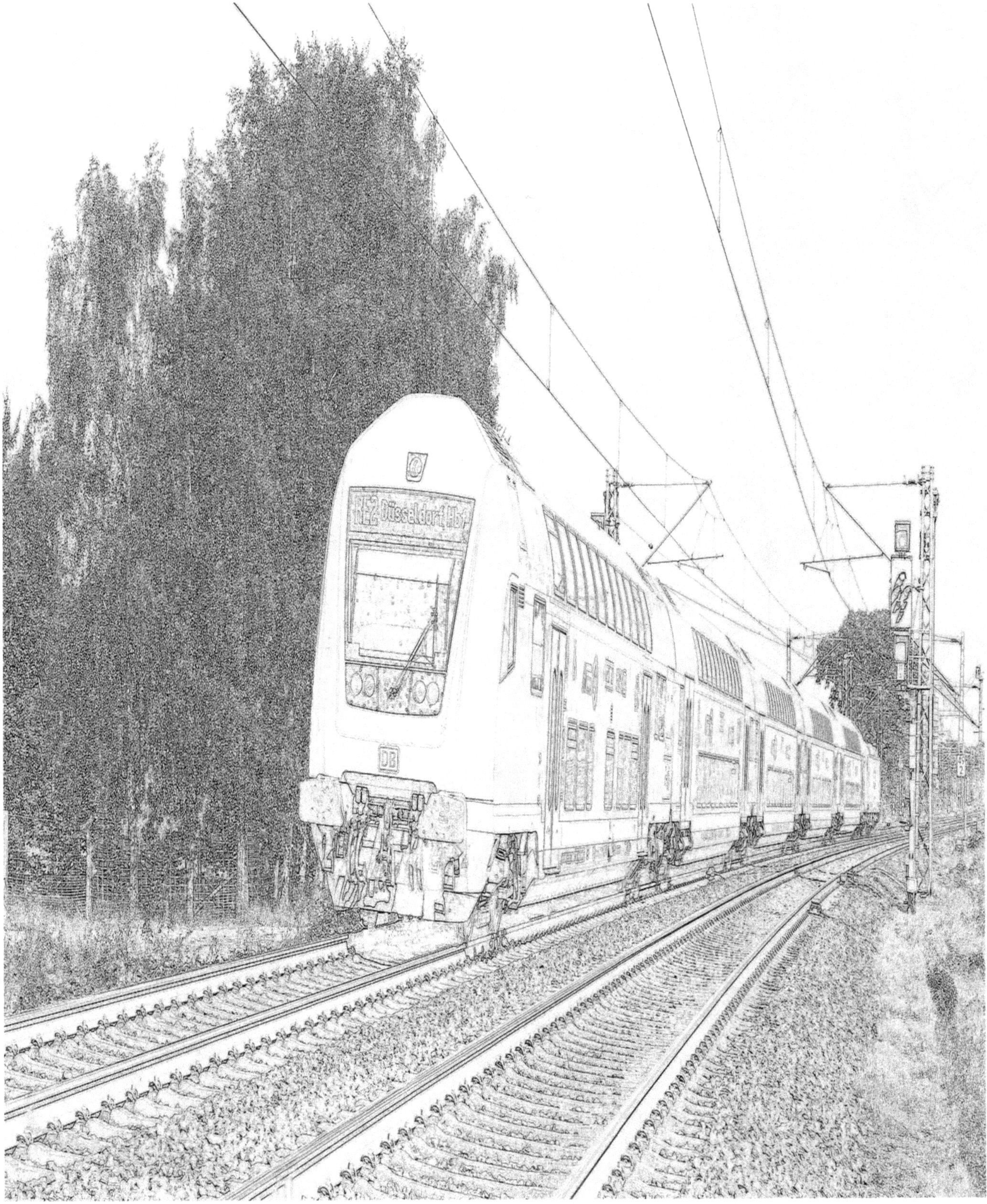
RE2 Düsseldorf Hbf

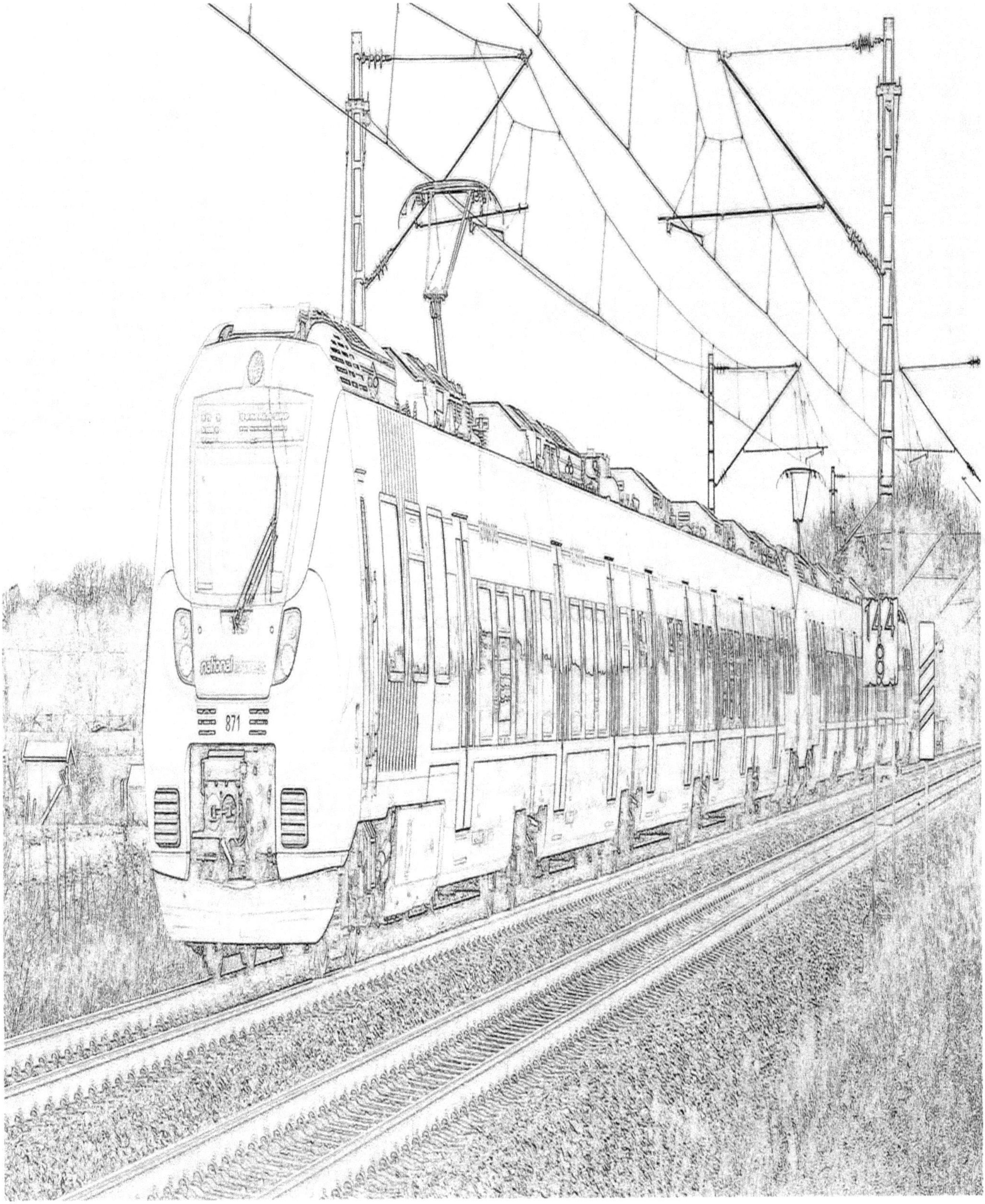
871
144
8

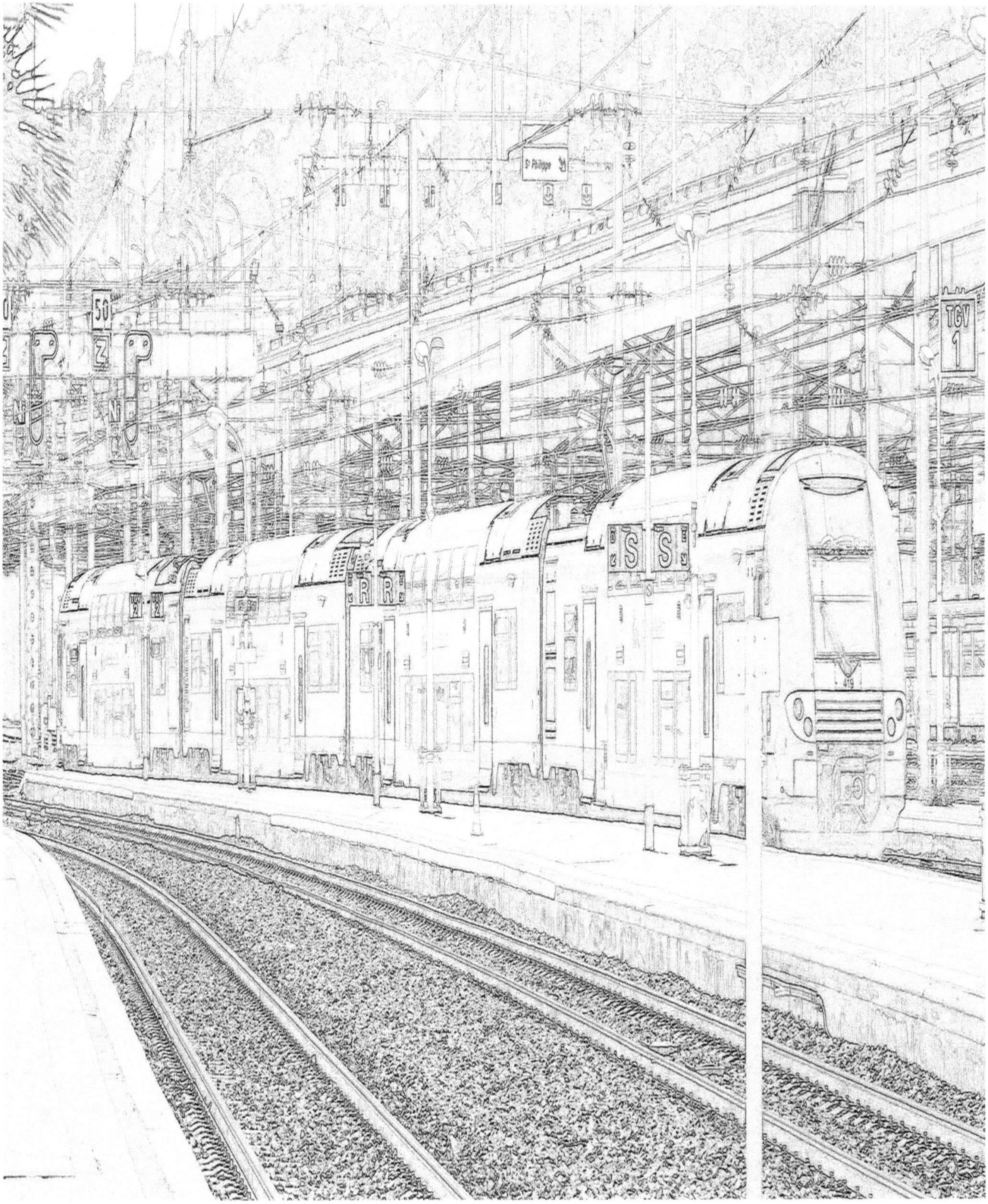
St Philippe
50
TGV
1
S S
R R

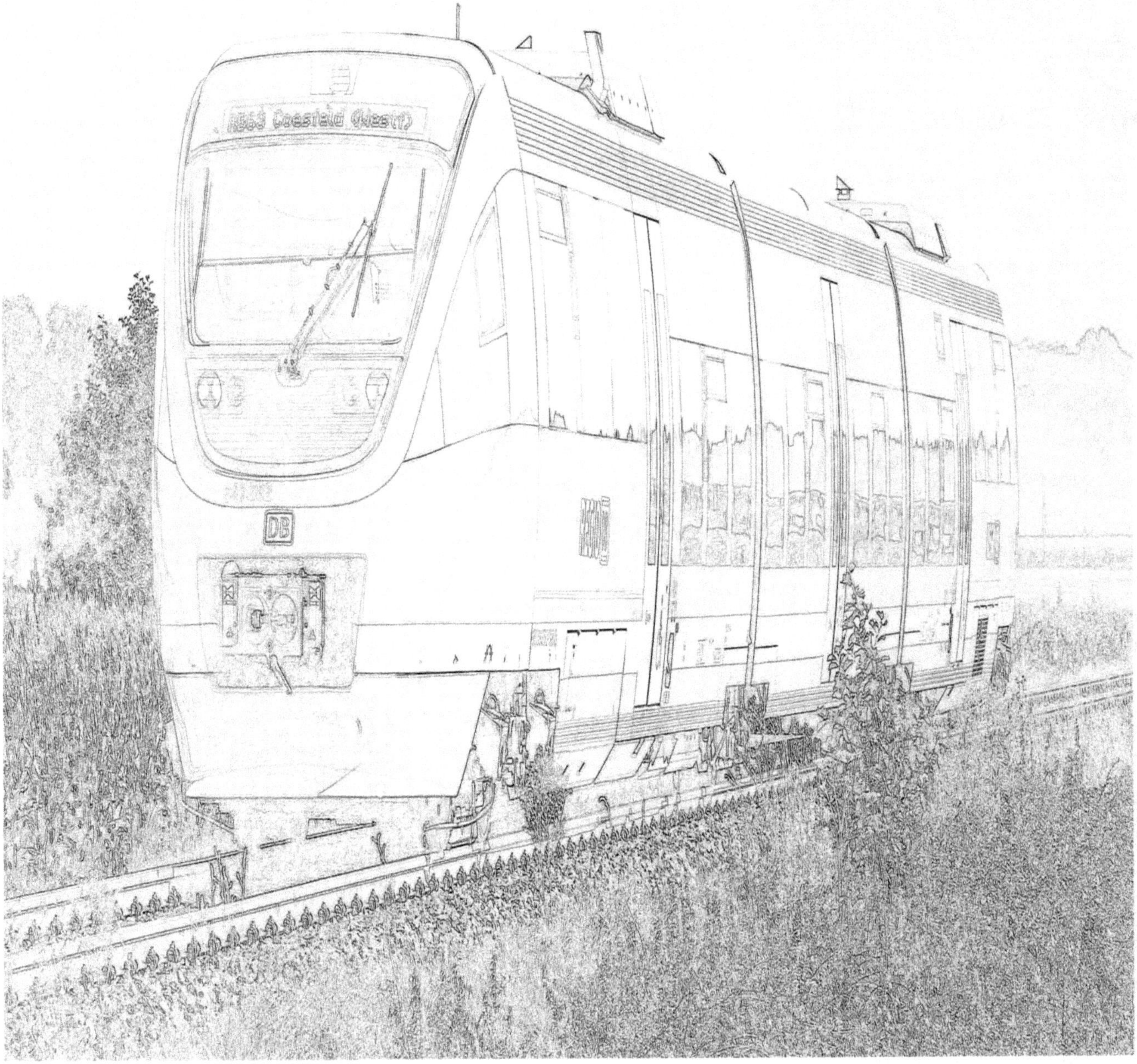
DB

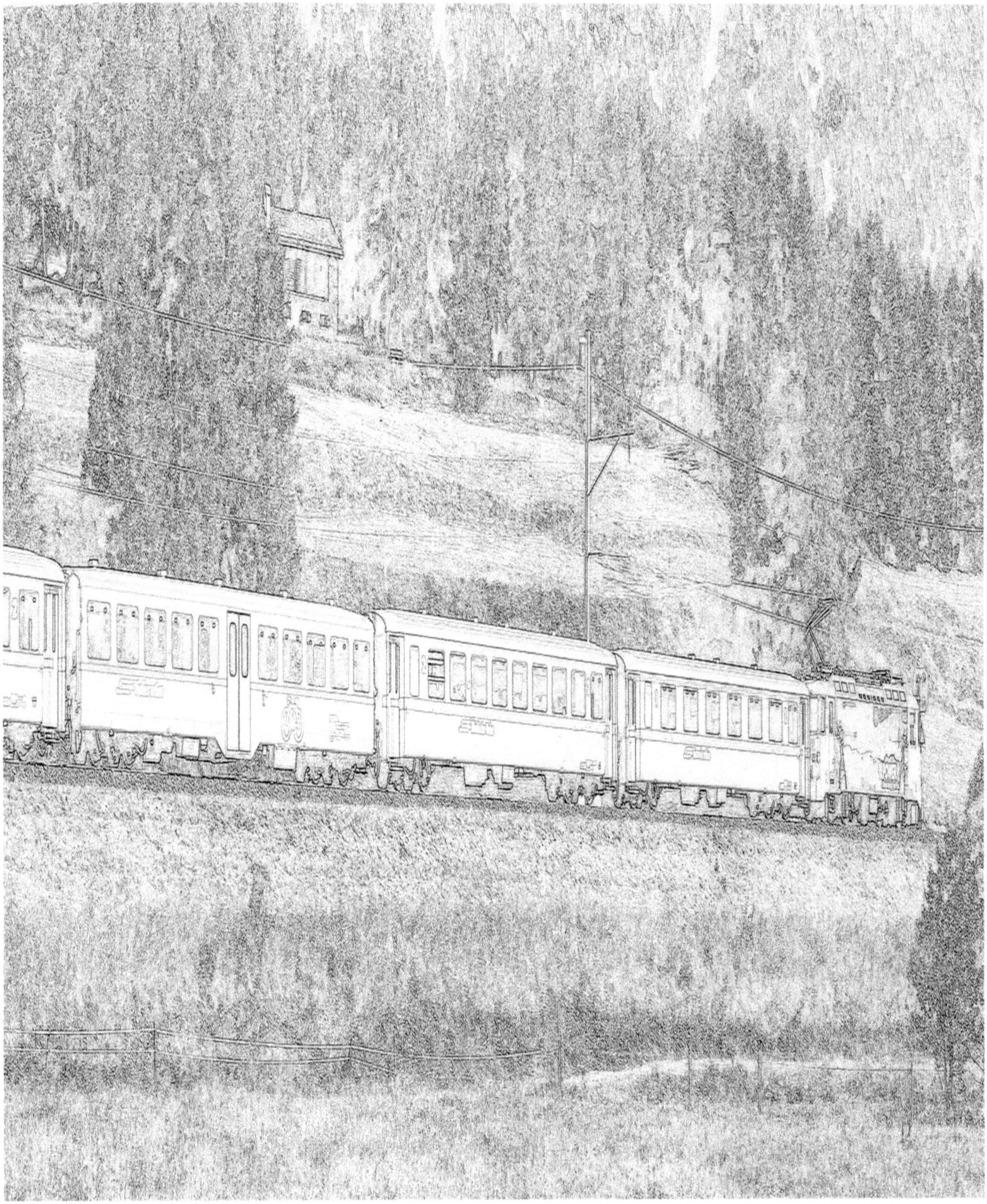

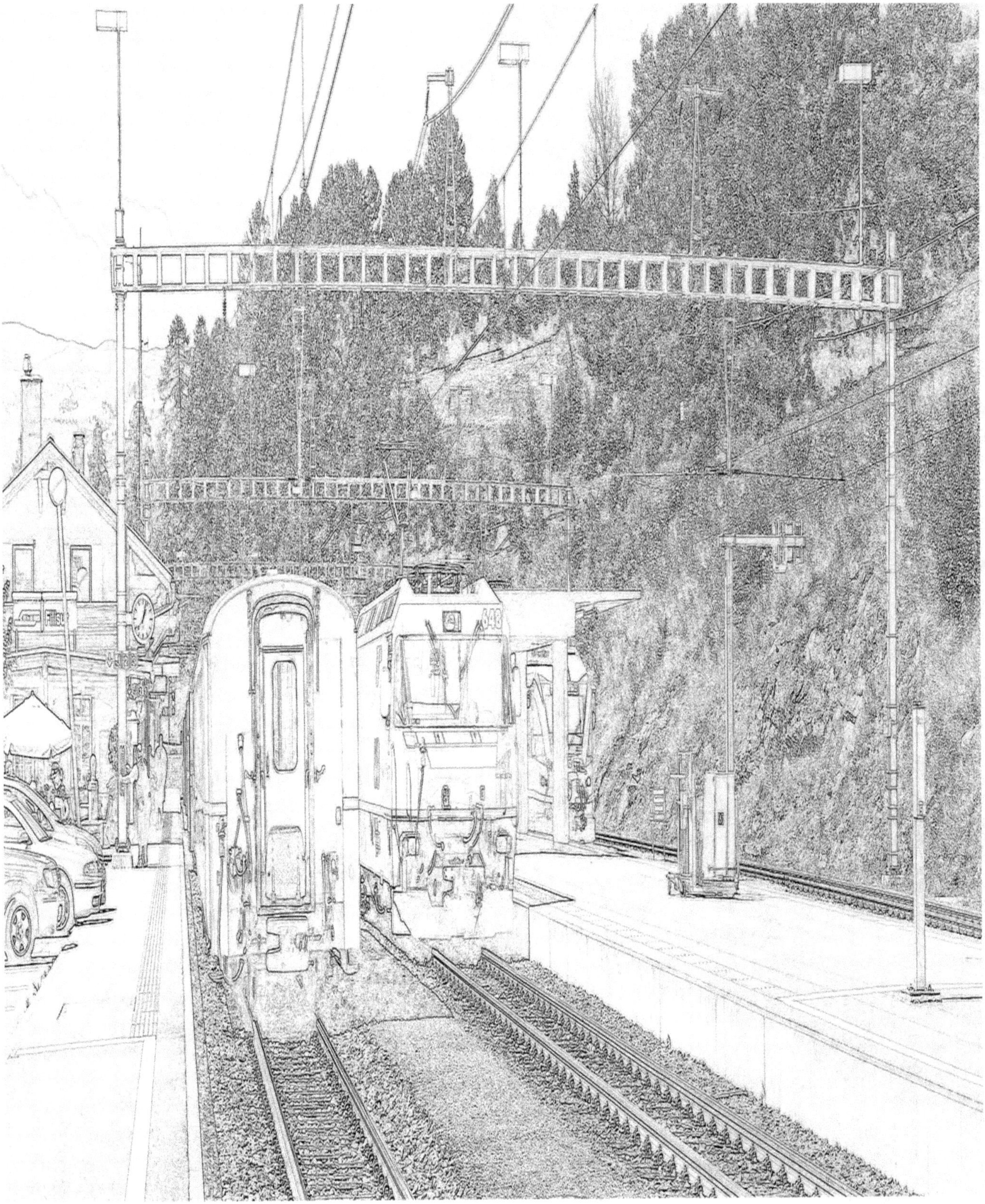
648

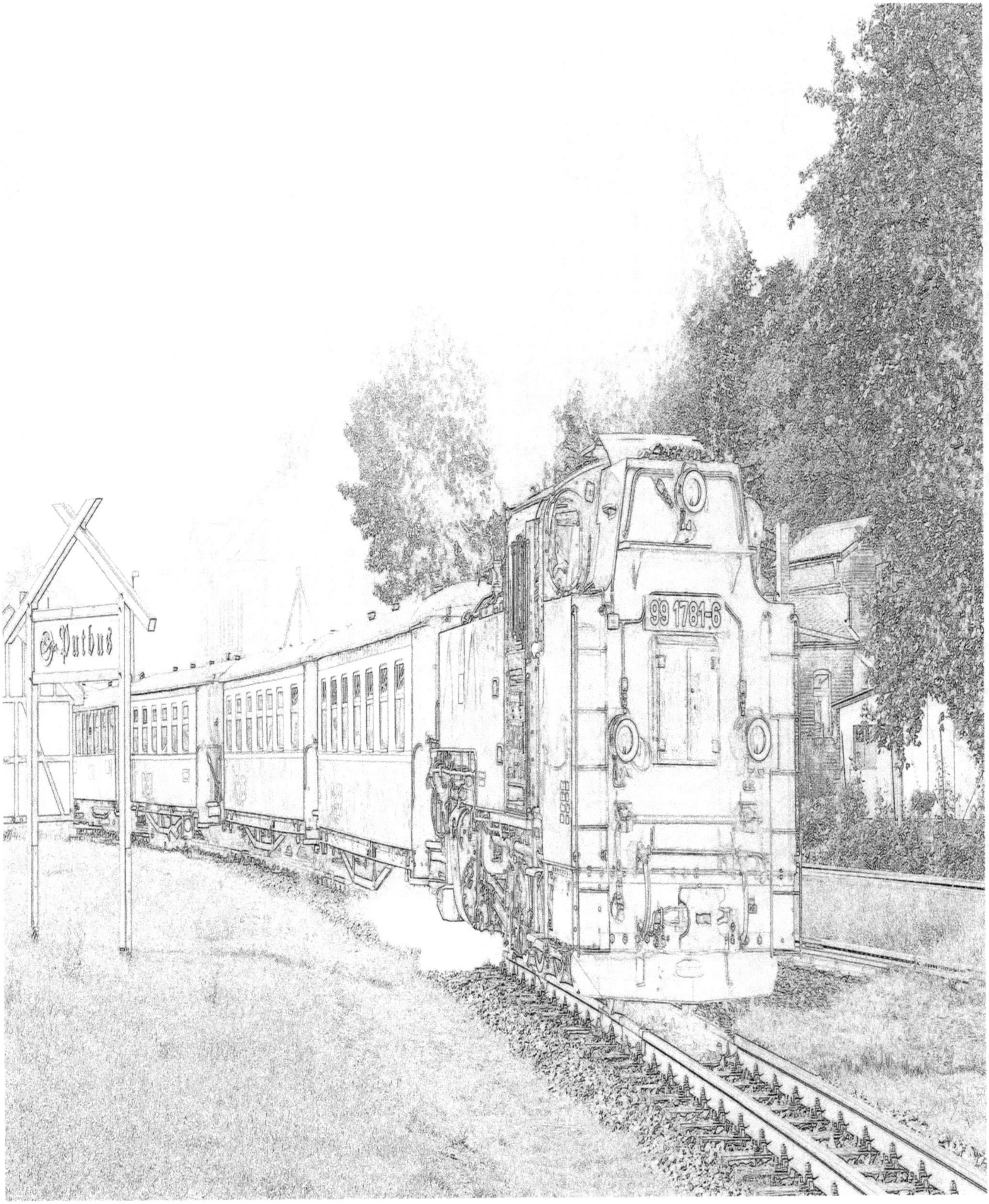
Putbus
99 1781-6

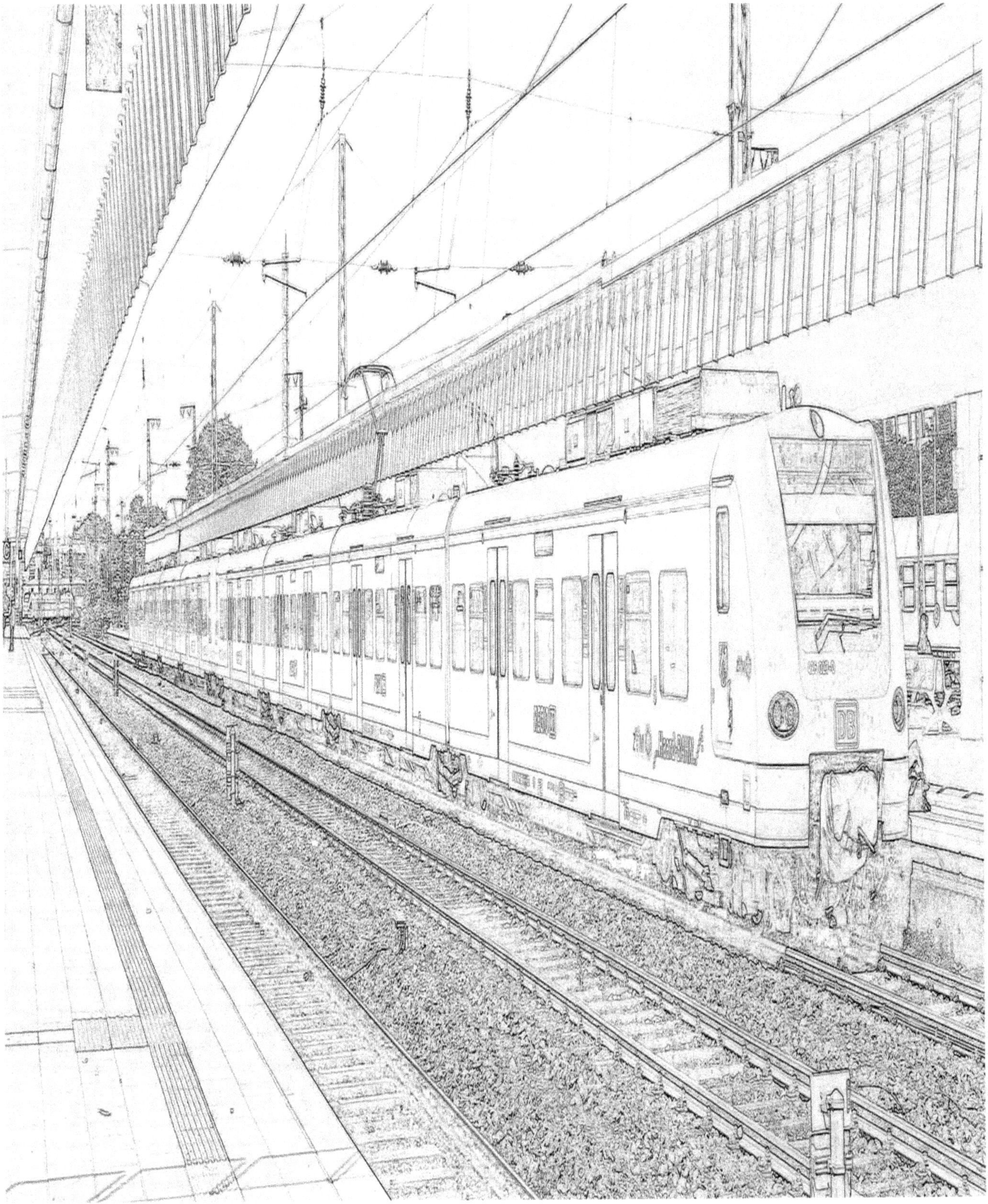

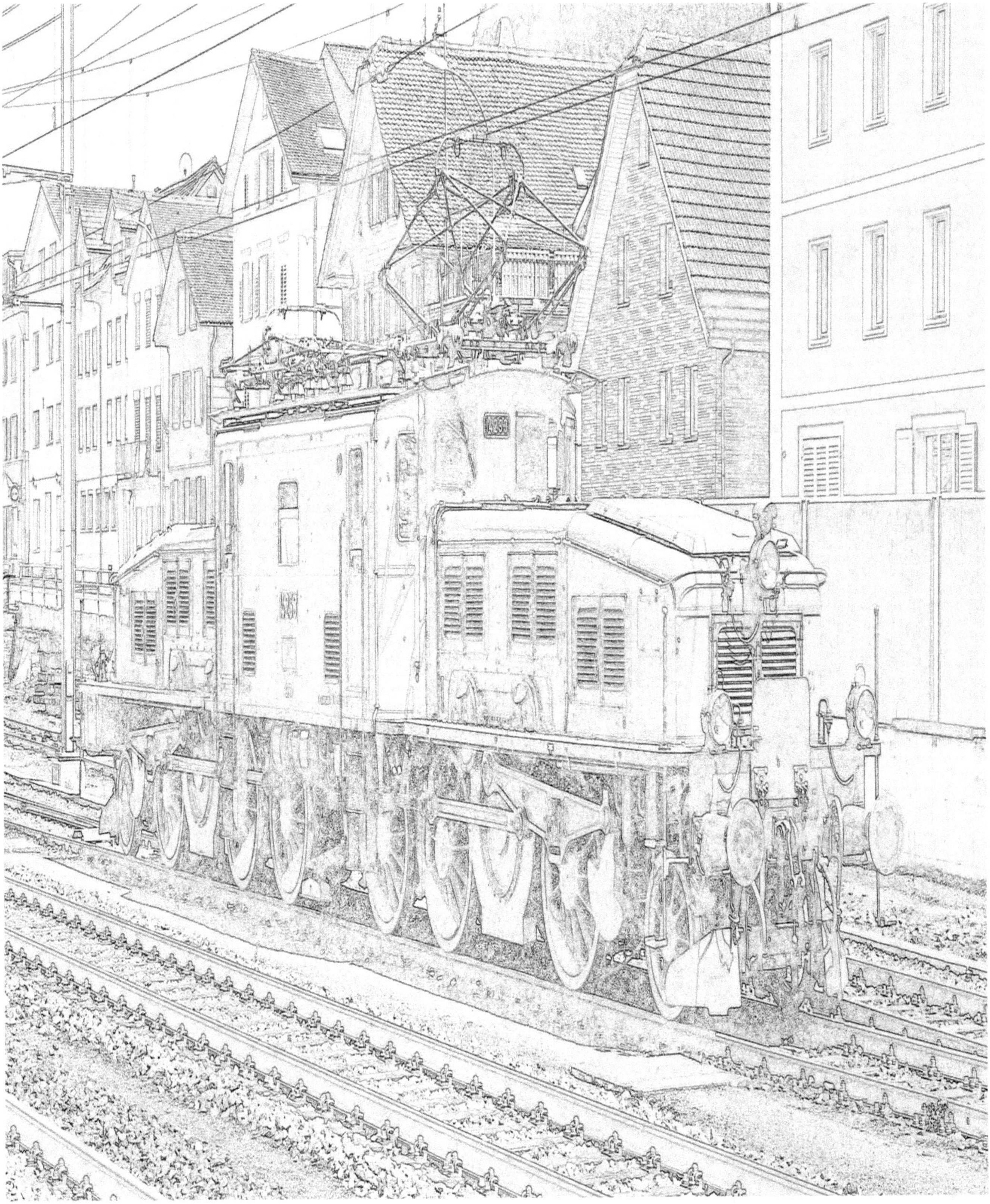

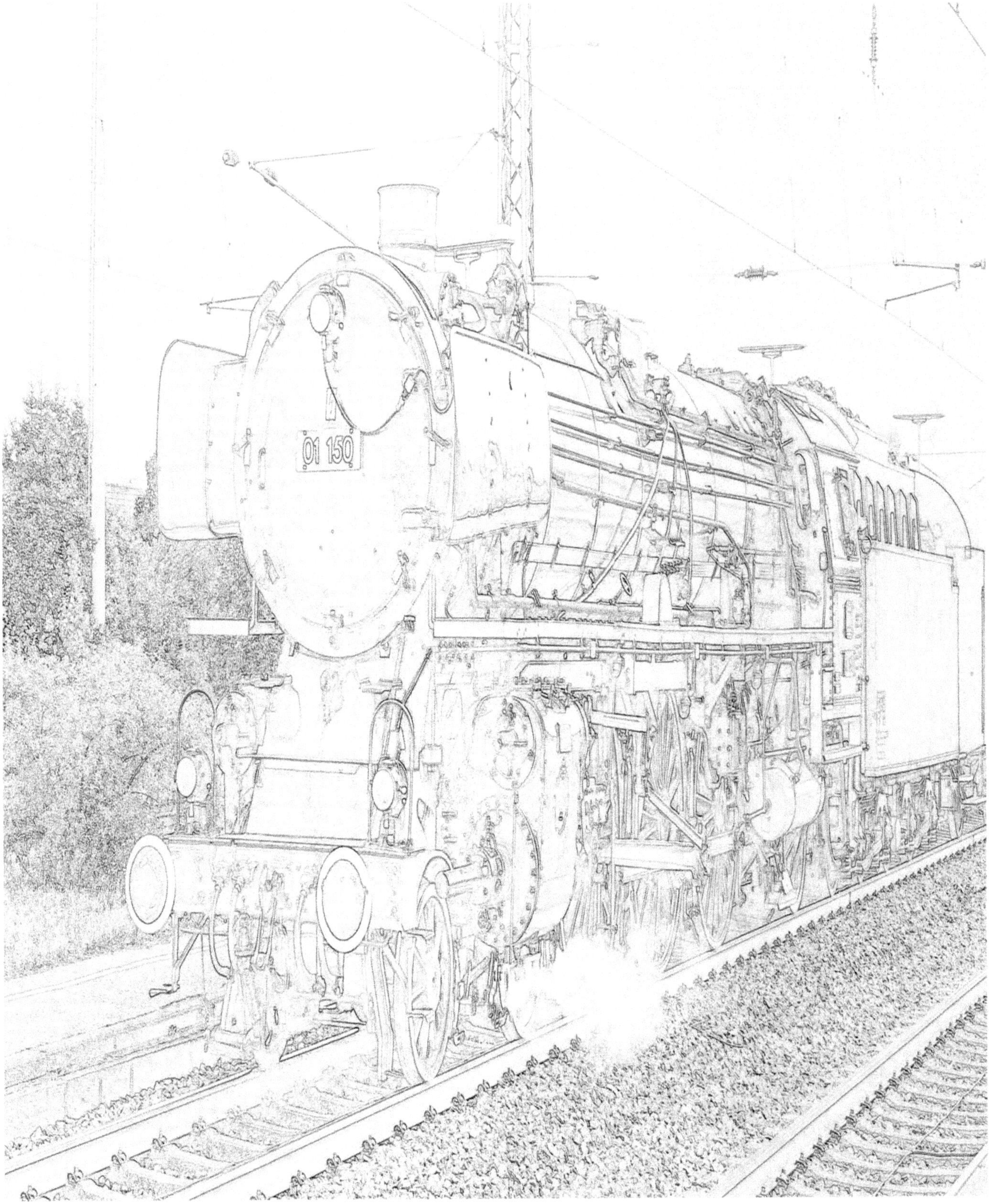
01 150

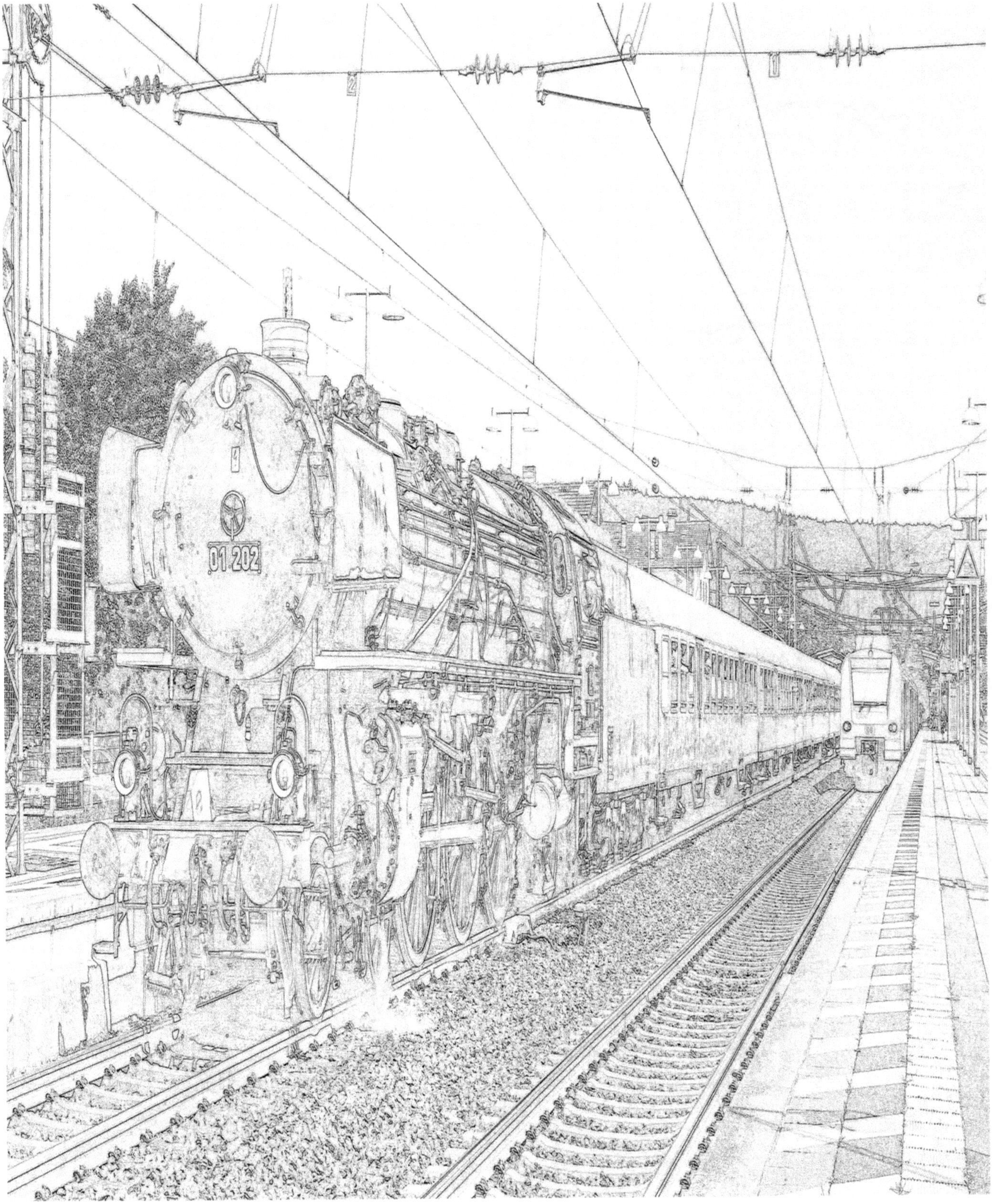
01 202

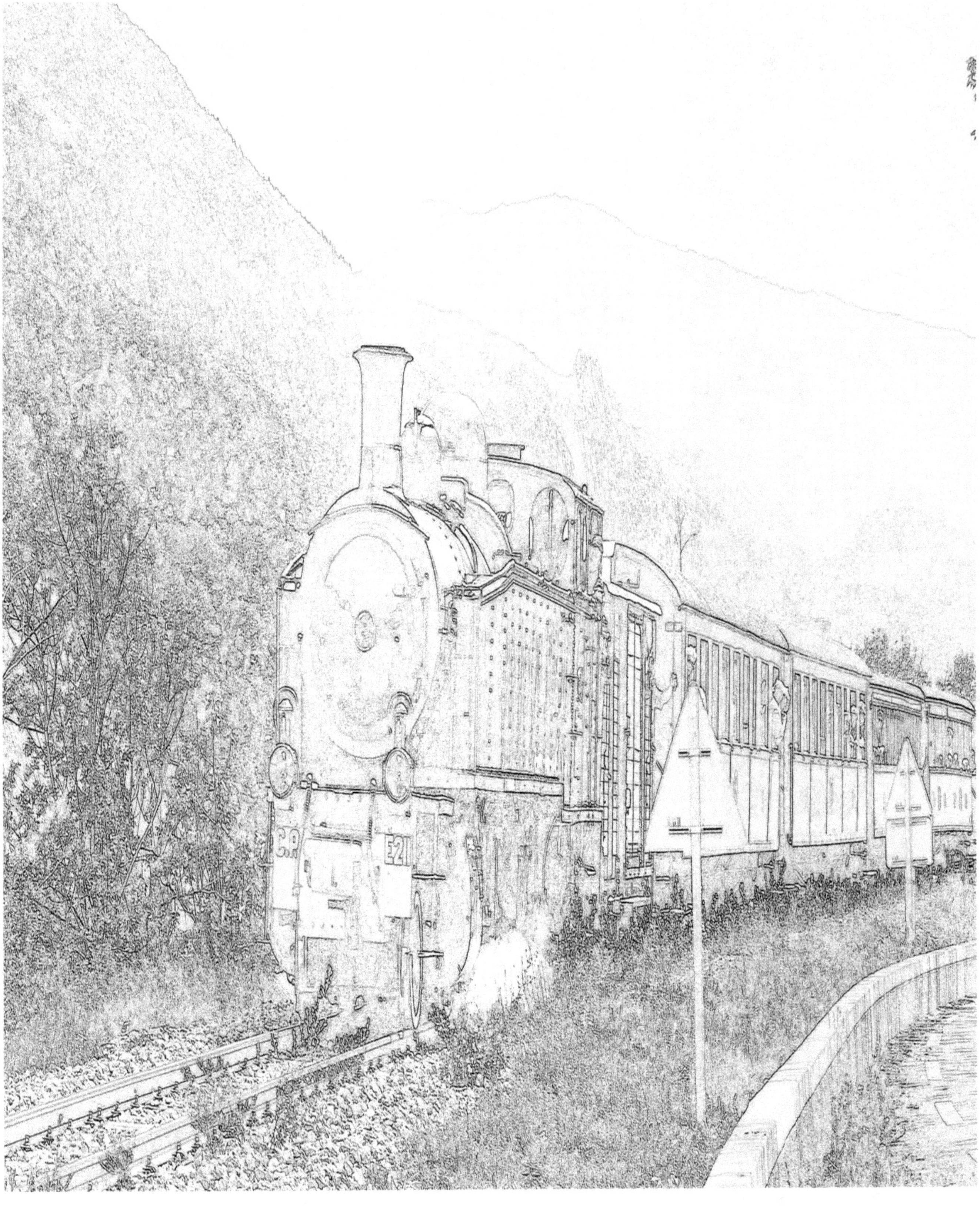
E21

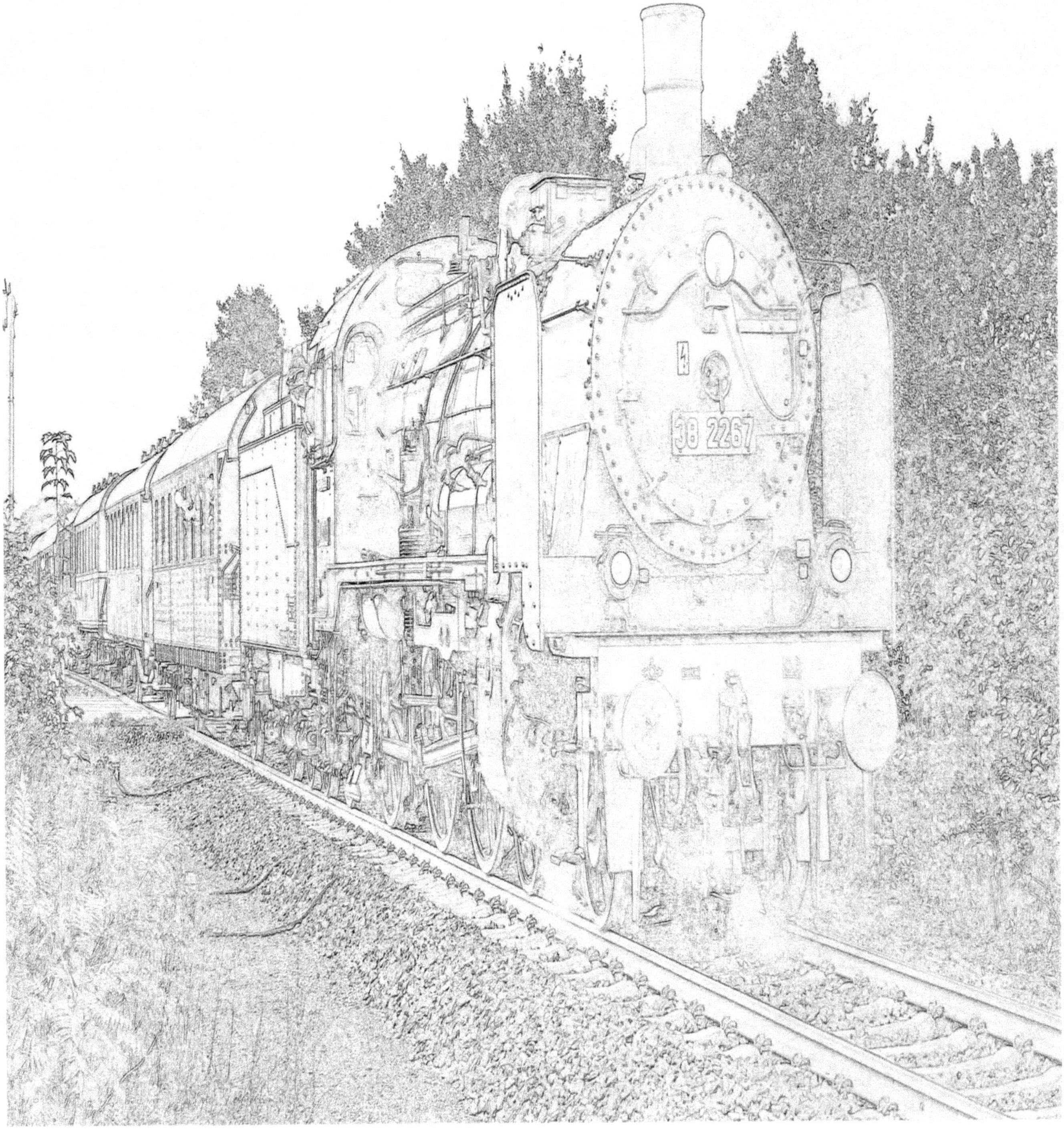
38 2267

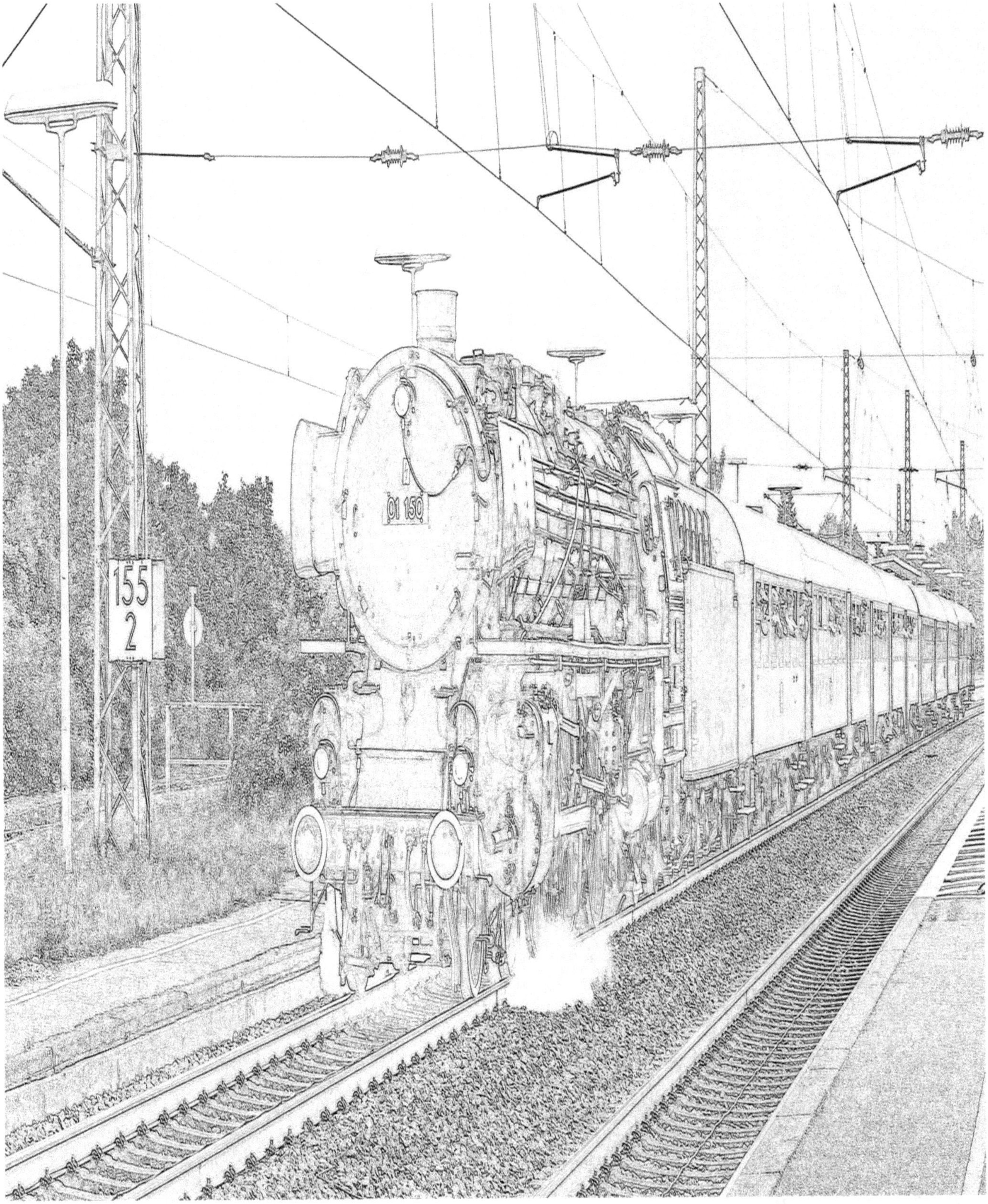
01 150
155
2

Thank you

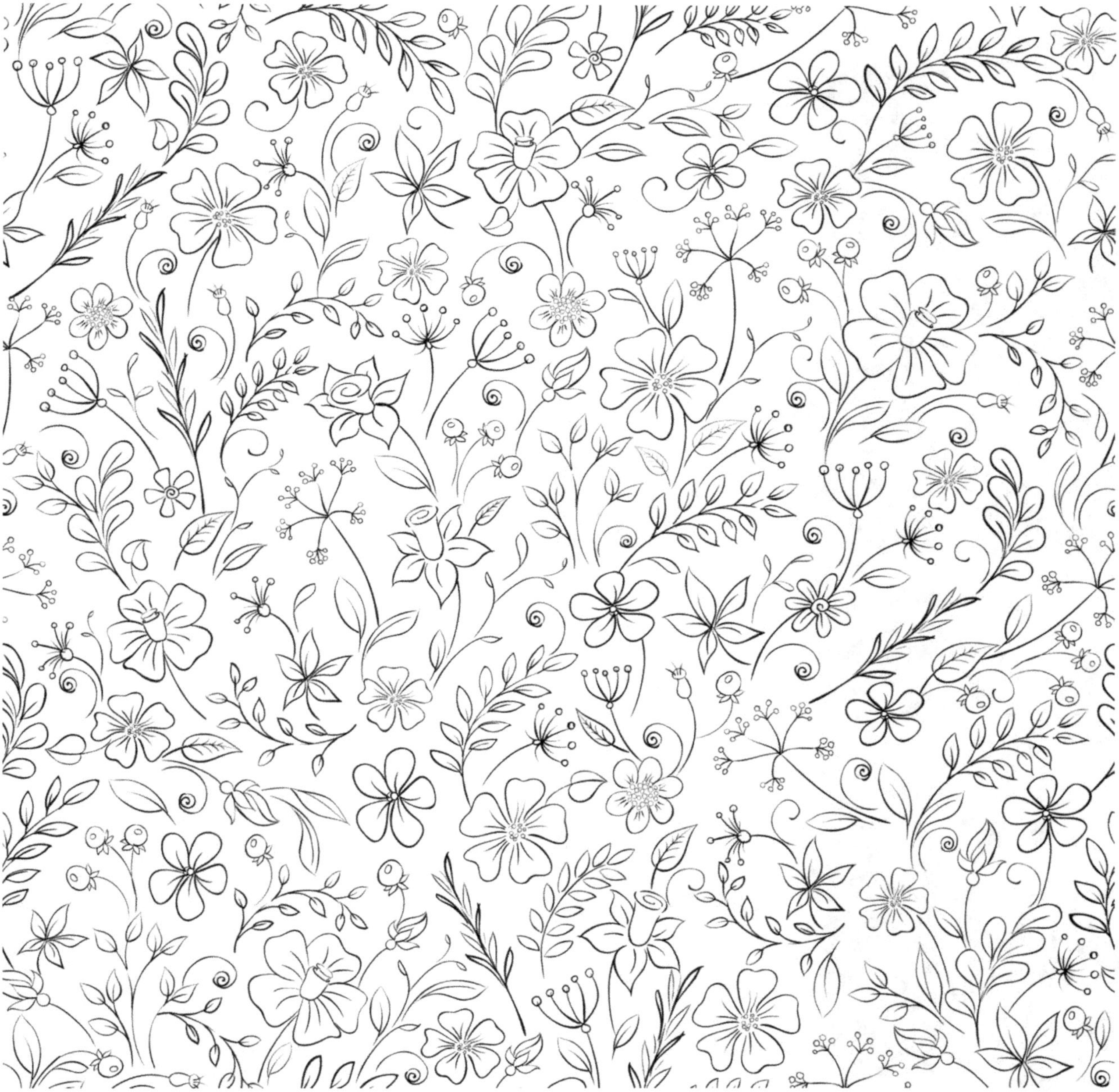

www.ingramcontent.com/pod-product-compliance
Lightning Source LLC
Chambersburg PA
CBHW081130180526
45170CB00008B/3058